D1425604

529 566 32 4

HOLI

By

Shalini Vallepur

BookLife
PUBLISHING

King's Lynn
Norfolk, PE30 4LS

Printed in Malaysia.

A catalogue record for this book is available from the British Library.

ISBN: 978-1-78637-805-7

Written by:
Shalini Vallepur

Edited by:
Madeline Tyler

Designed by:
Drue Rintoul

Photo Credits
All images are courtesy of Shutterstock.com. With thanks to Getty Images, Thinkstock Photo and iStockphoto. Front Cover – Olga_C. 2–3 – Kristina Sophie. 4–5 – StockImageFactory.com, Ruzely Abdullah. 6–7 – szefei, Claudine Van Massenhove. 8–9 – Sayan Nath, India Picture. 10–11 – reddees, Dipak Shelare. 12–13 – Dipak Shelare, pjhpix. 14–15 – StanislavBeloglazov, Akshat Khamparia. 16–17 – muratart, India Picture. 18–19 – reddees, India Picture. 20–21 – PI, StockImageFactory.com. 22–23 – Johnny Adolphson

CONTENTS

Words that look like this can be found in the glossary on page 24.

CELEBRATE HOLI WITH ME!

Holi Mubarak! That means 'Happy Holi' in my language, Hindi. My name is Ramya. I'm here to tell you about Holi.

Holi is a big festival that we love celebrating. It's full of colour and play. Come and celebrate with me!

HINDUISM

Holi is a festival that is part of a religion called Hinduism. Hinduism began in India over 4,000 years ago. We celebrate many festivals and follow lots of traditions as part of our religion.

Hindus believe in many gods and goddesses. Many gods make up the supreme god Brahman. Brahma, Shiva and Vishnu are some of these gods. They make up something called the trimurti.

HOLI

Holi is the festival of colour. We celebrate Holi every year in spring. Some years, Holi is in March and other years it's in February. The date changes because we wait for a full moon.

We do lots of fun things during Holi. We light bonfires and see our friends and families. Holi is special because there is a whole day of playing!

THE STORY OF HOLI

There once lived a king called Hiranyakashyap. He wanted everybody in his kingdom to worship him, but his son Prahlad did not want to.

Prahlad worshipped the Hindu god Vishnu instead of worshipping his father. This made Hiranyakashyap very angry and he wanted to punish his son.

The king asked his sister Holika for help. She was a demoness who had the power to touch fire without hurting herself. Holika took Prahlad and sat with him in the middle of a fire.

Holi celebrates and remembers that good always wins over evil.

The fire grew bigger and bigger. Vishnu protected Prahlad and saved him from being hurt. Holika died in the fire. Her power did not work because she had used it for evil.

BUILDING BONFIRES

There is a lot to get ready before Holi starts. People come together and build big bonfires around their city.

Bonfires can be made from twigs, leaves, coconuts and sometimes colourful things.

We put a doll of Holika on the bonfire too. Sometimes a doll of Prahlad is put on Holika's lap. We do this to remember how much Prahlad loved Vishnu.

HOLIKA DAHAN

Holi is usually two days long. Holika Dahan takes place on the first day. The bonfire is lit after sunset. We gather near the fire and chant mantras to scare away any bad spirits.

The doll of Holika is burned in the bonfire until it disappears. The doll of Prahlad is made of things that don't burn. Prahlad is unharmed, just like in the story of Holi.

PLAYING WITH COLOURS

The second day is all about playing! We take coloured powders called gulal and throw them in the air or smear them on our faces. The whole community gathers in the streets to play.

It doesn't matter how old you are or where you are from – everybody can play!

Prepare to be soaked! Gulal is mixed with water to make coloured water. We fill buckets with the coloured water and also shoot it out of water pistols called pichkaris.
Pichkaris

BHAJAN

Bhajan means holy songs. We sing and dance a lot during Holi. Some songs tell the story of the god Krishna and goddess Radha. Krishna is often shown to have blue skin. In the story, he uses colours to make Radha's face colourful like his own.

People also play the dholak. This is a type of drum. The streets come alive with colour, music, dancing and singing.

FESTIVE FOOD

When the playing is over, it is time for food. Everybody eats gujiya during Holi. It is a sweet dumpling that is filled with dried fruits and fried in oil.

We also eat lots of dahi vada. They are tasty lentil balls served with yoghurt and spices.

HOLI AROUND THE WORLD

Holi celebrations take place all around the world because there are many Hindus who live outside India. The largest Holi celebration outside of India is believed to take place in Utah, in the US.

I hope that you have learnt a lot about Holi! Why not see if there is a Holi celebration in your area?

GLOSSARY

community a group of people who are connected by something or live in the same area

demoness a female being that goes against the gods

mantras holy words or sounds that are sung or said in prayer

spirits beings that are not part of this world, such as a ghost or devil

supreme the greatest

traditions beliefs and actions that are passed down between people over time

unharmed not hurt

worship a religious act where a person shows their love for a god

INDEX